As one of the world's longest established
and best-known travel brands,
Thomas Cook are the experts in travel.

For more than 135 years our
guidebooks have unlocked the secrets
of destinations around the world,
sharing with travellers a wealth of
experience and a passion for travel.

Rely on Thomas Cook as your
travelling companion on your next trip
and benefit from our unique heritage.

Thomas Cook **pocket** guides

BRIGHTON

D0434532

Thomas Cook

Written by Debbie Stowe

Published by Thomas Cook Publishing
A division of Thomas Cook Tour Operations Limited
Company registration no. 3772199 England
The Thomas Cook Business Park, Unit 9, Coningsby Road
Peterborough PE3 8SB, United Kingdom
Email: books@thomascook.com, Tel: +44 (0)1733 416477
www.thomascookpublishing.com

Produced by Cambridge Publishing Management Limited
Burr Elm Court, Main Street, Caldecote CB23 7NU
www.cambridgepm.co.uk

ISBN: 978-1-84848-464-1

This first edition © 2010 Thomas Cook Publishing
Text © Thomas Cook Publishing
Cartography supplied by Redmoor Design, Tavistock, Devon
Map data © OpenStreetMap contributors CC–BY–SA; www.openstreetmap.org,
www.creativecomments.org

Series Editor: Karen Beaulah
Production/DTP: Steven Collins

Printed and bound in Spain by GraphyCems

Cover photography © Thomas Cook Publishing

CONTENTS

INTRODUCING BRIGHTON

Introduction..............................6

When to go 8

History.....................................10

Culture....................................12

MAKING THE MOST OF BRIGHTON

Shopping 14

Eating & drinking 16

Entertainment.........................18

Sport & relaxation..................20

Accommodation 22

The best of Brighton..............26

Suggested itineraries 28

Something for nothing.........30

When it rains............................31

On arrival.................................32

THE CITY OF BRIGHTON

Introduction to city areas 42

The city centre.........................44

The seafront.............................56

Around and north of
  Brighton Station...................67

OUT OF TOWN TRIPS

Lewes 80

East along the coast..............85

PRACTICAL INFORMATION

Directory..................................90

INDEX 94

MAPS

Brighton 34–5

Brighton city centre..............43

Brighton region 84

SYMBOLS KEY

The following symbols are used throughout this book:

@ address ❶ telephone Ⓦ website address ❷ email
Ⓛ opening times Ⓝ public transport connections ❶ important

The following symbols are used on the maps:

🄸 information office		O	city
➕ hospital		O	large town
🛡 police station		○	small town
🚌 bus station		=	motorway
🚆 railway station		—	main road
✝ cathedral		...	minor road
■ POI (point of interest)		—	railway
❶ numbers denote featured cafés, restaurants & venues			

PRICE CATEGORIES

The ratings below indicate average price rates for a double room per night, including breakfast:
£ under £70 **££** £70–120 **£££** over £120
The typical cost for a three-course meal, without drinks, is as follows:
£ under £15 **££** £15–25 **£££** over £25

❶ *Beach huts standing sentinel on the front*

INTRODUCING
Brighton

Introduction

London-on-Sea. England's San Francisco. However you choose to put it, there is no denying that Brighton is more than just a simple British seaside resort. This smallish south-coast town punches far above its weight, combining the knowing and sophistication of an urban hub with all the frivolous seaside joys beloved of the bucket-and-spade brigade.

Brighton's attitude and creativity are inescapable. Miscellaneous flyers festoon the town, each bearing glad tidings of another little piece of culture. At night, the sea breeze carries the strains of live music through the air, while mega-venues blare out the latest club tunes. The townsfolk channel the same spirit, from the proud LGBT (gay and allied) community to the sizeable student population to the bohemian denizens of North Laine. Add to that Brighton's urbane restaurant scene and a top-class museum and art gallery, and you're miles away from the typical English coastal town.

But there's another side to Brighton. Take a stroll along the iconic Brighton Pier, and all the cheesy seaside staples imaginable will unfold before you, from slot machines and sticks of rock to fortune-tellers, fairground rides and fish and chips. Both the pier and the famously stony beach are devoted to unalloyed fun, and their wide appeal transcends the demographics, with everyone from pensioners sitting and enjoying the view to children shrieking with delight on the roller coaster.

Brighton's attractions don't stop at the beach. The town is home to one of the most extraordinary-looking royal residences in the UK. A stunning melange of oriental influences, the Royal Pavilion, with its flamboyant domes, towers and minarets, is one of Britain's – not just Brighton's – most distinctive edifices. It is the perfect symbol of the *joie de vivre* and quirky individualism that pervade the city.

From the elegant cream Georgian town houses to the tacky neon lights of the pier, from artists' enclaves to the Donkey Derby, from a wild night on the town to paddling in the sea, Brighton's mix of urban cool, creativity and time-honoured coastal frolics will certainly convince you that you do like to be beside the seaside.

⬥ *The Royal Pavilion gardens*

When to go

SEASONS & CLIMATE

Although the town is by no means short of cultural highlights, an integral part of the Brighton experience is the joy of being by the seaside. This makes the weather a major factor in planning your trip. Owing to the vagaries of the British climate, warmth and sunshine are never a certainty, but as a guide, the city's main tourist season runs from around Easter to September. Outside that period some attractions close altogether, scale back or operate to reduced hours. This is not to suggest that the resort is not worth visiting at chillier times of the year – even though being windswept and rain-lashed on the pier does require a certain British stoicism or sense of humour.

Of course, warmer weather significantly boosts visitor numbers. If you'd rather not have to prowl the beach in search of a free spot or trail the streets to find a 'vacancy' sign in a B&B window, it might be wise to avoid absolute high season, which peaks with the August school holiday, at weekends throughout the summer months and at bank (public) holiday weekends. Brighton also does a lively conference trade, so check ahead if you don't want to find yourself blocked out of accommodation by hordes of Liberal Democrats, orthodontists or the like!

ANNUAL EVENTS

The town can also get busier during its main events, not that the extra crowds that they attract need put you off. Pick of the bunch is the Brighton Festival and Festival Fringe (ⓦ www.brightonfestival.org), which run concurrently for most of May. The Brighton Festival, said to be the largest multi-art form festival in England, features parades, outdoor shows, plays, music, literature and visual arts. The Festival Fringe (🅦 www.brightonfestivalfringe.org.uk) is an anything-goes version of the same thing. A thriving gay community means Brighton Pride (🅦 www.brightonpride.org), at the beginning of August, is another major spectacle. Brighton Live, a week of free gigs in September, and Burning the Clocks, a winter-solstice shindig, are among the city's other events, comprehensive details of which can be found on the council website (🅦 www.brighton-hove.gov.uk).

▲ *Celebrating Brighton's Pride*

History

Brighton did not become a major player in British history until the 18th century. It gets a mention in the Domesday Book (1086), when it was an insignificant fishing village known as Bristelmestune. However, assessed at five hides and a half, the rent was an impressive 4,000 herrings, and since the time of Edward the Confessor (1042–66) the town had soared in value from £8 12s to the princely sum of £12.

In 1514, French marauders torched the 'poore village in Sussex' of Brighthelmstone, as it was then known, destroying

◐ *Neptune detail over a doorway*

everything but part of a church and what would later become **The Lanes**. Thirty years later the spirited villagers fought off another attack by the French, sending the Gallic raiders fleeing to other parts of the south coast.

In the 1730s, local doctor Richard Russell hit upon what he deemed superior health properties in the seawater. On his advice, visitors began to flock to Brighton, which had by now shed its lengthy medieval monikers.

This fed into the incipient trend of seaside holidays, and Georgian houses now sprang up to cater to the well-heeled health-tourist set. Its most eminent member was the future George IV, who was advised by his physician that seawater would alleviate his gout. The then Prince Regent was such a fan that he spent long periods in Brighton in a rented farmhouse, enjoying some downtime from the pressures of royal life. He later had the place converted into what would become Brighton's most distinctive edifice, the Indian-inspired **Royal Pavilion**, whose safe distance from the capital made it an ideal spot for trysts with his mistress Maria Fitzherbert.

In 1841 the new railway line put Brighton within the reach even of non-aristocrats. Over the 19th century its population soared from 7,000 to 120,000, and many of the town's iconic buildings, including its two piers and the **Grand Hotel**, were constructed. Brighton began to sprawl, gobbling up nearby villages, and social housing quickly proliferated. However, recent gentrification has led the town to recapture the spirit of its glory days. It is now a fashionable place to live, King George's mantle having been assumed by many celebrities, who are in effect today's royalty.

Culture

Brighton is the cultural beating heart of Britain's south coast. So much is evident in its citizens, among whom are dreadlocked hippies, alternative types with a surfeit of tattoos and piercings, untroubled gay couples and legions of students. All reinforce the town's artsy individuality.

The fantastic **Brighton Museum & Art Gallery** is a splendid venue, with an absorbing mix of the old, the new and the stylish. Supporting it is a variety of other diverting museums, showcasing themes from the quintessentially Brightonian – slot machines and fishing – to toys and models and natural history.

The town's use as a location for some major British films – *Brighton Rock*, *Mona Lisa*, *Quadrophenia* – is in tune with its pioneering role in early UK film-making and cinematography. The theatre scene here is also healthy.

Art itself is huge, with a mind-boggling array of galleries throughout the town. The big date on the art calendar is the Artists' Open House, part of the Brighton Festival (see pages 8–9). But turn up at any time and art will be at your fingertips. A permanent hub is Brighton's Artist Quarter, on the seafront between the two piers, where fishermen's workshops have been converted into studios.

◗ *The derelict West Pier at sunset*

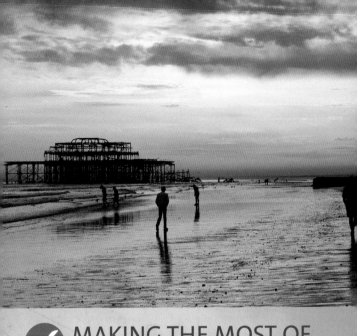

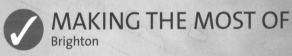

MAKING THE MOST OF
Brighton

Shopping

Retail opportunities to suit any proclivity can be found in Brighton. The town's quirky streak is manifest in copious individual boutiques; there are bargains for backpackers and students, and upmarket souvenirs for slightly more mature visitors with some cash to flash.

The most obvious shopping destination is The Lanes, a labyrinthine network of charmingly olde-worlde narrow alleyways between the Royal Pavilion and the **beach**. Jewellery, antiques and designer boutiques are nestled in among cafés and restaurants. The high-end wares appeal more to big-spending tourists, but the area is ripe for exploration even if you're just window-shopping, and conveys a fabulous sense of Brighton's history. The Lanes' warren-like nature makes getting lost somewhat inevitable, but it is all part of the fun.

North Laine is spelt differently and a different kettle of fish entirely. Lying to the north of The Lanes, it is far more bohemian, with students and hippies replacing moneyed mainstreamers. The jewellery most likely to be found on sale here is nose-rings. Tattoo parlours, vintage record stores, low-key, trendy cafés catering to vegetarians and the odd busker lend the district the air of a Camden-on-Sea.

Brighton's third atmospheric retail area is along the seafront, where trendy bars, tarot readers and fish and chip shops occasionally give way to the odd boutique, sometimes doubling as an artist's workshop. It's also a good place to pick up your kitschy beach inflatables.

If your retail needs are more practical, the **Churchill Square Shopping Centre** on Western Road, not far from the Clock Tower, offers the standard British mall experience, and the streets around it are also home to familiar retail names.

Bargain hunters should head for **Brighton Marina**, the local outlet shopping centre. As well as discounted clothes, accessories and other items, the facility has a plethora of entertainment options, not to mention some boats.

⬤ *North Laine*

Eating & drinking

Brighton offers two archetypal gastronomic experiences. The first is the British seaside staple of fish and chips, often truncated to fish 'n' chips. Not for the cholesterolly concerned, the dish consists of deep-fried, battered fish, typically cod or haddock, accompanied by chunky deep-fried potato chips. To this ensemble the diner may add salt, vinegar and sometimes ketchup. The seafront is chock-full of vendors, and the meal can be enjoyed at a table or sitting on the beach.

The second classic Brighton edible is rock, a confection of boiled sugar in the shape of a cylindrical stick. Typically brightly coloured and patterned, it often features the name 'Brighton' running vertically down its length. *Brighton Rock* is the title of Graham Green's famous novel of 1938. Rock is still going strong, unperturbed by the UK's various healthy eating drives.

As a popular getaway for weekenders and day-trippers, the town has a plethora of places to eat (the largest concentration of restaurants in southeast England outside the capital), from cheap and cheerful chippies to high-class purveyors of quality seafood. The city's restaurateurs have not rested upon their laurels: there are both stalwart Brighton eateries that have been serving up reliable cuisine for years, and newcomers with big ambitions, channelling the latest trends and ensuring food, presentation and ambience all impress.

The Lanes offers a wide choice of both restaurants and cafés, while North Laine has many casual outlets feeding a more alternative crowd. There are also plenty of places to eat along the seafront. Despite the town's party reputation, some eateries close earlier than you might expect, and during the week your restaurant choice will contract substantially after 22.00.

Aside from fish and chips on the beach, Brighton offers various pleasant spots for eating alfresco, weather permitting, such as the grassy areas of Old Steine and around, and Preston Park to the north. Supplies can be picked up from cafés or supermarkets.

◓ *Seafood for sale on the beach*

Entertainment

Graffiti (of the inspired, artistic variety rather than inane desecration), tables of vintage records set out on the street, quirky-looking boutiques – all this speaks of Brighton's creative vibe, which manifests itself in a vibrant and varied entertainment scene. Walk the backstreets and your vision will be constantly assailed by coloured flyers advertising the latest gig or comedy night.

The arts are celebrated here regularly and enthusiastically, both in the town's annual festivals and in its thriving nightlife, which reverberates to the sound of live music drifting out into the streets after dark. Though many of Brighton's live events are quaintly local, from time to time local celebrity DJ Fatboy Slim will pop up for the Brighton Big Beach Boutique, a huge seafront gig. Numerous late-night venues (the town is said to have over 300 pubs) bring in revellers from all over. When the sun goes down, carousers crawl from bar to bar and club to club, particularly around the seafront, Brighton's party hotspot. Known as Britain's gay capital, Brighton also has a flourishing LGBT scene to add to the mix.

For a small town (with a population of just over 150,000), Brighton boasts impressive arts venues – theatres and concert halls that would easily hold their own in a metropolis. Several theatres ply a decent trade here, with the discipline wholly suited to Brighton's provocative and creative nature. There are also plenty of places to catch a film, including at Britain's longest-functioning purpose-built cinema, the Duke of York's Picturehouse.

As well as simply keeping your eyes open for promising leaflets and posters around town, you can find details of forthcoming events through the *What's On Guide* (ⓦ whatson.brighton.co.uk), the *Brighton Magazine* (ⓦ magazine.brighton.co.uk), the *Brighton Source* (ⓦ www.brightonsource.co.uk) and the website ⓦ www.brighton.co.uk

🔺 *A seaside classic: the penny arcade*

Sport & relaxation

SPECTATOR SPORTS

It cannot plausibly be argued that Brighton & Hove Albion has the same cachet as, say, Manchester United or Liverpool. Nonetheless, the local football team (known as the Seagulls) has over a century of chequered history, having enjoyed a spell in the top flight and losing to Manchester United in an FA Cup final in the early 1980s, and in more recent years narrowly avoiding relegation from the Football League and liquidation. The Seagulls currently play at the **Withdean Stadium** but are planning to move to the Falmer Stadium in 2011. Tickets for games are available online or from the club box office. Withdean Stadium ⓐ 128 Queen's Road ⓣ 0845 496 1901

⬥ *At the Brighton racecourse*

ⓦ www.seagulls.co.uk ⓛ 09.30–17.30 Mon–Fri, 09.30–15.00 Sat match day, 09.30–14.00 Sat non-match day, closed Sun

Another popular day out is to **Brighton Racecourse**, where having a flutter on the horses and donning a fancy hat are all within the spirit of proceedings. Brighton Racecourse ⓐ Freshfield Road ⓣ 01273 603580 ⓦ www.brighton-racecourse.co.uk

PARTICIPATION SPORTS

The chilly sea temperature for much of the year has precluded Brighton's development as a full-on watersports destination. However, some hardy souls do take to the water, both for swimming and more high-octane splashing. Companies such as **Brighton Watersports** can provide equipment hire and lessons for aquatic pursuits from kayaking, stand-up paddle boarding and surfing to waterskiing and power boating. Some companies also offer fishing trips. Brighton Watersports ⓐ 185 King's Road Arches ⓣ 01273 323160 ⓦ www.thebrightonwatersports.co.uk ⓛ 10.00–19.00 or 20.00 daily (summer); 10.00–17.00 or 18.00 daily (winter), weather dependent

The most popular land-based pursuits tend to be at the extreme or quirky end of the sporting spectrum. Reverse bungee and crazy golf can usually be found, in high season at least, on the beach or pier. The latter's main leisure offering is, of course, slot machines, of which there is a cornucopia. In summer a modest fairground operates at the end of the pier. For a calmer time, luxuriate in a soothing spa (local hotels increasingly offer spa facilities) or head off to one of the villages around Brighton, where there are some beautiful walks (see pages 85–7).

Accommodation

While Brighton's classic form of accommodation is the bed and breakfast, the town has a range of options to suit the means of all comers, from backpackers to big spenders. A cluster of B&Bs can be found on and around Madeira Drive, with 'vacancy'/'no vacancy' signs in the windows. Kemptown, to the east of the town centre, offers many lower-cost options, while the upmarket establishments are clustered around Regency Square, west of the Churchill Square Shopping Centre. If you're a light sleeper, take note of any large clubs in the area, as there can be some noise when homeward-bound revellers spill onto the streets.

In low season, you can be fairly sure of finding somewhere to sleep on spec – unless you've overlooked a massive conference or similar. However, many places are booked out in summer and at weekends, so if you don't want to waste time traipsing from one fully booked place to another, it can be worth booking ahead. Most of the posher and larger establishments now have online booking systems, though for smaller, lower-budget options you have to call to reserve your room. Similarly, while most hotels now accept credit cards, some B&Bs may not, so checking is advisable. Prices may rise in high season.

Baggies Backpackers £ The comfortable basement music room and ground-floor TV lounge are among the plus points at this clean, well-equipped hostel, set in a roomy Regency house. Another is the rock-bottom prices. Visitors to Baggies repeatedly laud the friendly staff and sociable atmosphere. Sleeping

options include single-sex dorms, family rooms and a double.
ⓐ 33 Oriental Place ⓣ 01273 733740

The Grapevine £ Dormitory accommodation in a choice of
mixed or single-sex rooms. This friendly hostel in bohemian
North Laine also has Wi-Fi Internet. The sister outlet on the
seafront offers rooms sleeping up to four, and caters for stag
and hen weekends. ⓐ 29–30 North Road ⓣ 01273 777717
ⓦ grapevinewebsite.co.uk

Jurys Inn £ Situated close to the station, this reliable chain hotel
offers great value for money. Rooms are generously proportioned,
comfortable and tastefully decorated in warm shades. Service is
friendly and all rooms have high-speed Internet access. ⓐ 101
Stroudley Road ⓣ 01273 862121 ⓦ brightonhotels.jurysinns.com

Sheepcoat Valley Caravan Club Site £ Welcoming tents, caravans
and motorhomes throughout the year, this popular campsite
has a parent and toddler washroom and Wi-Fi Internet. It is
usually worth booking early. ⓐ East Brighton Park, north of
Brighton Marina ⓣ 01273 626546 ⓦ www.caravanclub.co.uk
ⓝ Bus: 1, 1A

Gulliver's ££ This elegantly decorated Georgian town house
offers impressive style and service for a reasonable price. There's
free wireless Internet and even a round-the-clock personalised
concierge service. Single rooms represent excellent value. The
nearby New Steine Hotel is affiliated. ⓐ 12a New Steine
ⓣ 01273 695415 ⓦ www.gullivershotel.com

Hotel Seattle ££ Simple, spacious and unfussy in style, rooms at this contemporary hotel come with extras, from the modern (Wi-Fi) to the traditional (home-made biscuits). It's all about clean lines and minimalism here: even the restaurant, which describes its menu as unpretentious modern British, is called Restaurant. ⓐ The Strand, Brighton Marina ⓣ 01273 679799 ⓦ www.hotelseattlebrighton.com

Paskins Town House ££ Green-oriented establishment which prides itself on having embraced environmental friendliness long before it was trendy to do so. Quirky Paskins has good-looking, individually decorated bedrooms and an Art Deco breakfast room. ⓐ 18–19 Charlotte Street ⓣ 01273 601203 ⓦ www.paskins.co.uk

Umi ££ Trendy three-star hotel with five types of room, some with sea views. Umi now has a restaurant, and offers half-board packages. ⓐ 64 King's Road ⓣ 01273 323221 ⓦ umihotelbrighton.co.uk

The Grand £££ This Brighton seafront institution is now in the hands of upmarket hotel group De Vere. Luxury touches like Egyptian cotton duvets add to the understated elegance, which is in harmony with the hotel's Victorian origins. ⓐ 97–99 King's Road ⓣ 01273 224300 ⓦ www.devere.co.uk

Hotel du Vin £££
This British boutique hotel chain is big on style and taste. Housed in Gothic Revival and mock-Tudor buildings in The

Lanes, it's also home to a classy bistro. Being where it is, parking can be a problem. **ⓐ** 2–6 Ship Street **ⓣ** 01273 718588 **ⓦ** www.hotelduvin.com

The White House Brighton £££

Highly reputed boutique B&B, the White House has won rave reviews for its laid-back affability, sleek rooms and value for money. The two tasteful single rooms have their own shower and basin but share a toilet. **ⓐ** 6 Bedford Street **ⓣ** 01273 626266 **ⓦ** www.whitehousebrighton.com

THATCHER, THE IRA AND THE GRAND

It was 1984, the middle of the Troubles – the violent political conflict over Northern Ireland. The Conservative Party top brass had checked into the Grand Hotel for their annual conference. Just before 03.00, as Prime Minister Margaret Thatcher was in her room, working on her speech for the following day's session, an explosion ripped through the building. The bomb, planted by an IRA member the month before, ultimately killed five people, but no government ministers. The next morning, in a 'Churchillian moment' that sent her approval ratings soaring, Mrs Thatcher opened the conference on time, declaring that 'all attempts to destroy democracy by terrorism will fail'. The hotel reopened two years later, with the prime minister in attendance, marked by a Concorde flyover.

THE BEST OF BRIGHTON

Brighton's compact size means that it is possible to pack a lot, including several iconic seaside experiences, into a short space of time.

TOP 10 ATTRACTIONS

- **Brighton Pier** Combining the glorious tackiness of the British seaside with splendid views and the giddy joy of being above water, the pier is a Brighton must-do (see page 59).

- **Beach** It may not be sandy but the town's trademark shingles do little to dent enthusiasm for eateries, bars, fortune-tellers and crazy golf (see page 58).

- **Fish and chips** Slosh on the vinegar and shake over the salt before tucking into the staple seaside feast (see page 16).

- **The Lanes** The ridiculously picturesque warren of passageways that hark back to medieval times, offer retail and dining at their most atmospheric (see page 46).

- **North Laine** Alternative, artistic and bursting with attitude, this funky area is the spiritual home of anyone who's a hippie at heart (see pages 67–8).

- **Brighton Museum & Art Gallery** Newly redeveloped and brimming with verve, runs the gamut from world art to fashion, with an absorbing section on the town's history (see page 49).

- **Royal Pavilion** Boasting Indian and Chinese influences, the eye-poppingly majestic pavilion, once a future king's love nest, is now Brighton's landmark building (see pages 46–7, 49–50).

- **Brighton Festival & Fringe Festival** Creativity abounds at the city's annual arts jamboree (see pages 8–9).

- **South Downs** England's green and pleasant land is at its best in the surrounding villages, all rolling hills and gambolling sheep (see pages 85–8).

- **Fishing Quarter** Tourism might win out over authenticity, but the seafront is still quaintly pleasant (see page 58).

🔻 *Sunset on the pier*

Suggested itineraries

HALF-DAY: BRIGHTON IN A HURRY

Unless the weather is truly abysmal, it would be a pity to come to Brighton without taking a walk along the pier and beach, possibly stopping to eat on the seafront. The Lanes are the other must-see, and present numerous dining options. If the weather's too inclement for spending several hours outside, forget the seaside stuff and slot in a visit to either the Royal Pavilion – which you should view from the outside in any case – or Brighton Museum & Art Gallery if you're on a budget.

1 DAY: TIME TO SEE A LITTLE MORE

Given a full day, you can comfortably fit in all of the above, climatic conditions allowing. There's also time to head north from The Lanes and stop for a snack or some shopping in the cool North Laine district. If you're in Brighton overnight or catching a late train out, it's well worth taking in some late-night entertainment, be it a play at one of the theatres, some stand-up, live music or a club night.

2–3 DAYS: SHORT CITY BREAK

In this more leisurely time frame, you can really enjoy the beach – as ever, weather permitting – taking the time for a long stroll, some sunbathing or even some watersports. As well as doing all of the above at a more relaxed pace, you can incorporate other town-centre attractions: the Sea Life Centre if you're with children; Volk's Electric Railway to enjoy the coastal views without the walking; and your pick of the town's museums, which focus on such varied themes as fishing, historic slot machines, and toys and models. There is also time to visit a couple of attractive churches and to enjoy the city's green spaces, Preston Park (and Preston Manor) to the north and Old Steine in the centre. You can also have your fill of Brighton's nightlife. But if you find yourself yearning for the pastoral, take half a day to see some of the charmingly rural South Downs villages nearby, or take the short trip to historic Lewes, just 11 km (7 miles) to the east.

LONGER: ENJOYING BRIGHTON TO THE FULL

As well as allowing you to tick off all the major town highlights with ease, a longer sojourn lets you fully explore the area around Brighton, with bus trips to the local villages that also offer the allure of delightful walks in the South Downs countryside. There's also the opportunity to venture into interesting outlying neighbourhoods, such as Kemptown, east of the town centre, or Hove, to the west.

🔺 Brighton's famous pebble beach

Something for nothing

Provided that the weather is suitable, many of Brighton's best bits come at no cost. Both the beach and the pier can be enjoyed free of charge – provided you're not tempted by the slot machines or fairground rides at the end of the pier. Discovering The Lanes also costs nothing – again, assuming you stick to window-shopping. The astonishing architecture of Brighton Pavilion can be admired without paying the entrance fee, and that puts you in the vicinity of Brighton Museum & Art Gallery, for which there is no charge, and which could easily mop up a few hours. If you are feeling energetic, walking in the South Downs is another way to make the most of the area on a limited budget.

Should your visit coincide with a date in Brighton's festival calendar, there will be further opportunities for entertainment without paying a penny. Some Brighton Festival & Fringe Festival events are free, for instance, and the splendid spectacle of Brighton Pride is also open to all.

When it rains

British seaside towns can be notoriously depressing when it rains, but Brighton has plenty to ensure that no trip will be a total washout. Even the pier has plenty of dry areas, in the form of dedicated amusement arcades, indoor places to drink and eat and covered benches where sea views can still be enjoyed without a drenching. If the rain looks likely to be more than a brief downpour, head for the Pavilion area, located just a short walk from Brighton Museum & Art Gallery. It's possible to while away the wet hours in this pair of top attractions and not get soaked travelling between the two.

Family groups – or fish fans of any age – could head to the Sea Life Centre, which is fascinating enough to keep you both entertained and dry for quite a while. Several buildings of note in Brighton and around – Preston Manor, Anne of Cleves House in Lewes, and Charleston farmhouse in Firle – are also good for a wet day. Brighton is also packed with top-quality eateries and cosy cafés (many with Wi-Fi Internet), where killing time is no hardship.

On arrival

ARRIVING BY AIR, RAIL, ROAD

The nearest useful airport to Brighton is London Gatwick. (Shoreham, or Brighton City, Airport does not handle scheduled flights.) At just 40 km (25 miles) away, Brighton is an easy 30-minute drive from London Gatwick. Direct trains also take around half an hour, with fares starting from as low as £5 if booked in advance. Frequent coaches, which are usually the cheapest way to travel, especially if you cannot book far ahead, also make the trip, taking 45 minutes.

Luton Airport, which handles cheap flights, is also on a direct rail link to Brighton, but it is on the other side of London, and the journey takes about two hours, even with no changes. It's also considerably more expensive, with fares north of £25. The journey by coach takes twice as long and can cost a similar sum. Again, advance booking can result in savings. Travelling by car from Luton Airport, via the M1, M25, M23 and A23, takes about two hours, depending on time of day and density of traffic.

Many visitors pitch up in Brighton by train. The station is conveniently situated for all the main areas of interest to tourists, at the top of Queen's Road, which segues into West Street as it continues south towards the seafront. The main accommodation clusters are all just about reachable on foot, but if you don't fancy the walk there is a taxi rank and numerous buses run between the station and the town centre. The station itself is modern and pleasant, with outlets of Smiths and Marks & Spencer, other snack kiosks and ATMs. Outside, on

Terminus Street, are several pleasant cafés which handily show train departure and arrival times on television screens.

The city's bus hub, Pool Valley Coach Station, directly south of Old Steine, is even more central, but like many bus garages, it's not as swish as the average train station. Nonetheless, its location cannot be beaten for convenience.

The A23 links London and Brighton, running as far as it is possible to go – right down to Brighton Pier. Several one-way systems have been instituted in Brighton over the years, which can be tricky to navigate efficiently if you're not familiar with them. Parking is often difficult and expensive, with prime spots near the main sights usually taken, and high charges in NCP car parks. A park-and-ride system operates from Withdean Stadium, which is convenient if you're driving but don't want the stress of finding parking in the town centre.

FINDING YOUR FEET

Being small, Brighton is relatively easy to adjust to, and presents no major safety issues that do not apply to any other UK town. However, as in any town centre, the atmosphere can sour rapidly at pub and club 'kicking-out time', particularly on a Friday or Saturday night. The main clubs may have a police presence outside, and foreign visitors unused to the Northern European drinking culture may be surprised and alarmed by the scenes of drunken degeneracy that sometimes unfold. As in many urban seaside party towns, there is also something of a drugs subculture in Brighton, so the young and hip-looking may be approached by dealers. However, they are unlikely to linger if you make it plain that you're not interested.

ORIENTATION

Two main thoroughfares trisect Brighton from north to south: Queen's Road, which begins at the railway station and runs down to the west of The Lanes, where it becomes West Street; and the A23, which enters the town as London Road and undergoes several name changes before ending up as Old Steine at Brighton Pier. Many of Brighton's attractions lie on or just off this latter thoroughfare.

The town is impressively well signposted, with the number of minutes' walk to each destination also helpfully indicated. Brighton's trickiest spot to get a course-plotting handle on is The Lanes, whose tortuous crisscrossing defies easy navigation, but that is part of their charm. The area is small enough – and bordered by clearly contrasting roads – that you're unlikely to veer too far off course.

There are a few useful landmarks. The obvious one, which should prevent even the hopelessly navigationally challenged first-timer from getting too lost, is the sea. If you are close to the seafront the relatively frequent glimpses of water you'll get as you cross the streets that slope down to the English Channel should give you at least an approximate idea of whether you are heading in the right direction. Another useful orientation point is the Clock Tower, while the Dome and Pavilion are also quite unmistakable.

Ethical Brighton is a highly pedestrian-friendly city. Three of its top tourist draws – the pier, the beach and The Lanes – are entirely car-free. And other major places to visit, such as Brighton Museum & Art Gallery and the Royal Pavilion, are set in pedestrian-only complexes. Some of the town's large

◆ *Brighton railway station*

thoroughfares can be difficult to cross owing to their width and the high levels of traffic that ply them. However, there will always be a designated pedestrian crossing in the vicinity, even if you have to take a slight detour to reach it.

GETTING AROUND

The majority of Brighton's highlights are within easy walking distance of each other, and with the railway and bus stations also nearby it is quite possible to spend your stay in the town without recourse to public transport of any kind. Maps and signposts are plentiful; the former can be downloaded from the town's official website (ⓦ www.visitbrighton.com). Some of the joy of Brighton is the quirky sights on the streets, which is another argument for spending at least some time exploring on foot.

Public transport in the town is provided by buses. As elsewhere in the UK, bus travel is not as cheap as might be expected, the standard single fare being just under £2. However, a short journey or tourist fare between some of the main attractions costs only £1, and there are CitySAVER and Super Save tickets which can be decent value if you're going to be making a lot of journeys or going day-tripping – the tourist office can sell the latter at a discount. Taking a bus is also the only way to see the outlying villages if you don't have your own set of wheels. The system is very high-tech, and passengers can send a text to find out bus times from a particular stop. If you're not travelling on a day pass, pay the driver when you board. If you're heading for Lewes, you have the choice of either the bus or the train. As is usually the case, it's quicker by train but cheaper by bus. ⓦ www.buses.co.uk

⬥ Volk's Electric Railway

A quicker and more convenient, but of course more expensive, way to get around is by taxi. There are taxi ranks at East Street and Queen's Square, and cabs can also be hailed in the street around the Clock Tower.

As might be expected, a town as student-orientated as Brighton is guaranteed to be fairly cyclist-friendly. It is one of five British towns specially chosen by the government to promote cycling, and it has cycle routes that form part of the National Cycle Network. One designated cycle route runs east to west along the seafront. Bike hire is also available through the tourist office (see page 93).

CAR HIRE

Though driving is a convenient means of reaching your destination, the town's compact nature and costly, restrictive parking mean that there is little benefit in having a car once you arrive. But if you're intending to explore any of the surrounding villages and beauty spots, being liberated from reliance on public transport will be welcome. Should you wish to hire a car for the purpose, all major rental companies are represented in Brighton.

Avis Ⓦ www.avis.co.uk
Budget Ⓦ www.budget.co.uk
Europcar Ⓦ www.europcar.co.uk
Hertz Ⓦ www.hertz.co.uk
National Ⓦ www.nationalcar.co.uk
Sixt Ⓦ www.sixt.co.uk
Thrifty Ⓦ www.thrifty.co.uk

▶ *Deckchairs facing the sun on the pier*

 THE CITY OF
Brighton

Introduction to city areas

The town centre, what might be described as the heart of Brighton, is just set back from the seafront. It is the warren of alleyways, known as **The Lanes**, that form the centrepiece of this district; teeming with charming eateries and boutiques, they provide for pleasant wandering. This central area also includes the grassy complex that is home to three big-hitting sights grouped closely together: the **Royal Pavilion**, **Brighton Dome** and **Brighton Museum & Art Gallery**.

Brighton's **seafront** easily merits its own section. Not only does this area incorporate the beach and iconic **Brighton Pier**, but the beachfront arcades also house shops and eateries of all descriptions, as well as fortune-tellers and a great variety of entertainments. There are also several flagship buildings and other attractions.

Further inland, a third area begins at **North Laine** and extends north past the train station, as far as **Preston Park**. Although it's at a slight remove from the main action, there are several good reasons to venture away from the sea on all but the most flying of visits.

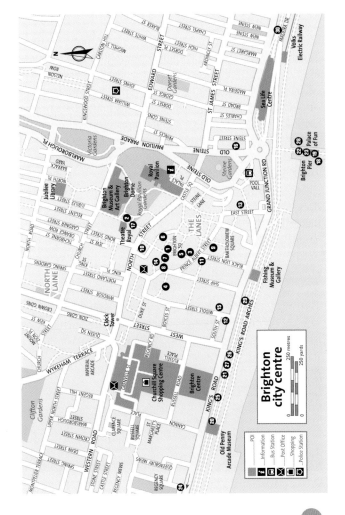

The city centre

Brighton's compact city centre enjoys an enviably high density of points of interest; indeed, there can be few British cities where so many distinctive attractions are clustered together so conveniently. The main museum and gallery (under the same roof), architectural marvels, historic edifices, entertainment venues and atmospheric retail district sit cheek by jowl in and around the town's so-called Cultural Quarter. Even if you wandered randomly you couldn't roam too far without hitting a place of note. There's also a decent complement of green spaces. They – and the presence of the sea not too far away – ensure that Brighton's heart never feels too overwhelmingly urban or remotely polluted.

⬤ *The stunning interior of the Dome*

There really is no better way to get around the centre of Brighton than on foot. Nothing in this part of the town is more than a few minutes' walk from anything else (unless you lose your bearings in The Lanes!). All major points of interest are extremely well signposted, with the time taken to reach them on foot often included. Even if you do veer off course, Brighton's Georgian town houses and brightly coloured terraces make the occasional inadvertent detour a pleasure.

SIGHTS & ATTRACTIONS

Brighton Dome

Though you're unlikely to be able to gain access to the interior unless you're there for a cultural event or conference, the Dome is near enough to the other top draws in Brighton's Cultural Quarter to justify stopping by to admire it. Built over 200 years ago, the Dome originally housed the future King George IV's horses. Architect William Porden drew inspiration for its bold design from paintings of India, and Georgian naysayers were amazed that the building didn't collapse when the scaffolding was removed. ⓐ 12A Pavilion Buildings, Castle Square ⓣ 01273 700 747 ⓦ www.brightondome.org

Clock Tower

As flagship Brighton constructions go, the Clock Tower may be dwarfed by some of its more ambitious rivals, but this wonderfully ornate landmark still deserves a look. One of a series of commemorative timepieces erected under the British Empire in honour of various royal birthdays, the pink granite and limestone tower dates from 1888, the year after Queen Victoria's Golden Jubilee. At the bottom are portraits of the then royal family between corner limestone statues. The gilt copper globe at the top once moved up and down to mark the half hour and hour before being stilled and silenced after protests from long-suffering residents. ❷ Junction of West Street and Queen's Road

The Lanes
The pedestrianised warren of alleyways that developed from the old fishing village of Brighthelmstone affords a delightful glimpse into Brighton's history. Though the incursion of modernity in the form of designer boutiques and cafés with Wi-Fi was inevitable, many of the buildings retain their 18th-century features and some of the businesses are long-standing concerns. Allowing yourself to get lost exploring this utterly charming quirky time capsule of a district is one of Brighton's joys. ❷ Area between North Street, Ship Street, Bartholomew Square and East Street

Royal Pavilion
Sticking out like an exquisite sore thumb, Brighton's iconic royal residence must be one of the most incongruous and admired landmarks in the country. It was originally a (relatively) humble farmhouse, which the then Prince of Wales rented for sojourns in his beloved Brighton. The future monarch later commissioned John Nash (the architect of London's Regent Street, who also remodelled Buckingham Palace) to redesign the place. Nash didn't hold back. Today's visitors are astounded by a staggering infusion of oriental domes, minarets and pagodas that would sit more harmoniously in the exotic Far East than

they do in Sussex. ⓐ 4/5 Pavilion Buildings, off Pavilion Parade and
Castle Square ❶ 03000 290 900 ⓦ www.royalpavilion.org.uk
🕒 09.30–17.45 daily Apr–Sept, 10.00–17.15 daily Oct–Mar, last
admission 45 minutes before closing ❶ Admission charge

Old Steine

This pleasantly leafy space – the former village green – offers
welcome respite for a mid-shopping or sightseeing sit-down,
especially as the nearest main park is about 2 km (over 1 mile)
from the town centre. The centrepiece of the neatly kept square
(though, along with the war memorial section, it actually forms
more of a tear shape) is the impressive Victoria Fountain. In
warm weather Old Steine's benches are a popular place to kick
back and enjoy the greenery and architectural views all around.
ⓐ North of Brighton Pier, to the east of The Lanes

⬥ *Regency costumes at the Brighton Festival*

CULTURE

Brighton Museum & Art Gallery

Running the gamut from 5th-century Peruvian drinking vessels to a shirt belonging to Norman Cook (Fatboy Slim), the town's splendid flagship cultural institution is a bold, bright and modern venue to which it is well worth dedicating a few hours. The wide-ranging museum section covers all manner of themes, and never strays into over-worthy territory. The Fashion & Style gallery starts with Regency trends and runs to replica mod, skinhead, rocker, skater and hippie outfits. Elaborate costumes from Burma, the Caribbean and West Africa are

ABBA'S BRIGHTON BREAKTHROUGH

In 1974, four Swedish musicians were enjoying moderate chart success at home and fighting for that elusive break. Agnetha Fältskog, Anni-Frid Lyngstad, Björn Ulvaeus and Benny Andersson had recently decided to name their act using their initials. Hoping that international song competitions might be the breakthrough they sought, the group applied, not for the first time, for the Eurovision Song Contest and performed 'Waterloo' at Brighton Dome. Abba's catchy disco riffs and platform boots took the world by storm. Their Brighton victory – the track is widely held to be the best Eurovision song ever – led to UK and US success and a European tour from which the foursome never looked back.

highlights of the Performance gallery. The human body and ancient Egypt are also covered, and there's an absorbing section on Living in Brighton. It's all very interactive, with flaps to lift, fabrics to touch and a Punch and Judy show to stage. A seat in the shape of a hand and a sofa resembling a pair of lips are among the highlights of the 20th Century Decorative Art & Design gallery. Fine, world and modern art are all represented. The facility is fully wheelchair-accessible. ⓐ Royal Pavilion Gardens ⓣ 03000 290900 ⓛ 10.00–17.00 Tues–Sun, closed Mon except public holidays

RETAIL THERAPY

Even the most reluctant of shoppers will surely enjoy retail as it is in The Lanes, thanks to their inviting atmosphere. Shops in this part of the city tend to be high-end, with several long-established jewellers, antique shops and designer boutiques. As conventional as The Lanes are special, the **Churchill Square Shopping Centre** (ⓐ Western Road ⓛ 09.00–18.00 Mon–Wed, 09.00–20.00 Thur, 09.00–19.00 Fri & Sat, 11.00–17.00 Sun) has the usual mainstream mix of British high-street names, which extend on to the surrounding streets.

The Antique House Spread over two floors of one of the oldest buildings in its street, the stock here – from works of art to bits and pieces for the home and upmarket period pieces – is constantly rotated. ⓐ 43 Meeting House Lane ⓣ 01273 321684 ⓦ www.theantiquehouse.co.uk ⓛ 10.00–17.00 Tues–Sat, 12.00–16.00 Sun, closed Mon

Choccywoccydoodah Boasting a name that Willy Wonka himself would be proud of, this local company crafts mostly Belgian chocolate into stylishly tempting upmarket designs. They also do fancy cakes. ⓐ 27 Middle Street ⓣ 01273 329462 ⓦ www.choccywoccydoodah.com ⓛ 10.00–18.00 Mon–Sat, 11.00–17.00 Sun

Gold Arts Fabergé, Links of London and Pandora are among the brands glittering away at this bling-filled store. Certificated diamonds are a speciality, but second-hand jewellery and watches can also serve as a less high-spending girl's best friends. ⓐ 7 Brighton Place ⓣ 01273 776000 ⓦ www.goldarts.co.uk ⓛ 09.30–17.00 Mon–Sat, 12.00–16.00 Sun

Montezuma
Posh chocolate emporium, where the delectable brown stuff takes the form variously of truffles, dainty dollops, bars and blocks, and cooking or drinking chocolate. Set up after the founders' confectionery epiphany on a trip to South America, this Brighton-based concern has also spread to other cities. ⓐ 15 Duke Street ⓣ 01273 324979 ⓦ www.montezumas.co.uk ⓛ 09.30–18.00 Mon–Sat, 11.00–17.00 Sun

Sheridan Cooper's Wine Cellar A newcomer to The Lanes, these people know their onions – or rather grapes – when it comes to plonk. There are special offers, and often tastings on Saturdays. ⓐ 21 Prince Albert Street ⓣ 01273 730445 ⓛ 12.00–19.00 Tues, 11.00–19.00 Wed–Sat, 12.00–16.00 Sun, closed Mon

TAKING A BREAK

Angel Food Bakery £ ❶ The smell is nigh-on irresistible at Angel, whose gorgeous-looking cupcakes can be gorged upon at the window counter, while you enjoy a coffee and some people-watching. ⓐ 20 Meeting House Lane ⓣ 01273 208404 ⓦ www.angelfoodbakery.co.uk ⓛ 10.00–18.00 Mon–Sat, 11.00–17.00 Sun

Zafferelli £ ❷ Though some bristle at the service charge, this decent Italian eatery serves up standard trattoria fare at astonishingly low prices. Pizza and pasta are often available for less than the cost of a typical Brighton sandwich. ⓐ 31–32 New Road ⓣ 01273 206662 ⓦ www.zafferelli.com ⓛ 12.30–14.30, 17.30–22.30 Sun–Thur, 12.30–14.30, 17.30–23.30 Fri & Sat

Food for Friends ££ ❸ Dine in understated style on meat-free Mediterranean, Middle Eastern and North African delights. Food is fresh, local, vegetarian and seasonal – ethical eating at its finest. Book ahead. ⓐ 17–18 Prince Albert Street ⓣ 01273 202310 ⓦ www.foodforfriends.com ⓛ 12.00–22.00 Sun–Thur, 12.00–22.30 Fri & Sat

TFI Lunch ££ ❹ A quiet spot in The Lanes, with outside tables and friendly staff. As the name suggests, the eatery serves the usual lunchtime fave, such as sandwiches, toasties, paninis, wraps, salads and jacket potatoes. There's also a reasonably priced all-day breakfast menu. ⓐ 10 Dukes Lane ⓣ 01273 325945 ⓦ www.tfilunch.com ⓛ 08.30–16.30 Mon–Fri (summer),

08.30–15.30 Mon–Fri (winter), approximately 09.00–17.00 Sat, 10.00–16.00 Sun, trade dependent

Tictoc Café ££ ❺ Tictoc oozes friendliness, from the fair-trade coffee to quirky décor, including a photo of the Fonz on the wall. The fare includes Belgian hot chocolate, soup, smoothies, cakes, salads and sandwiches. There is also Wi-Fi Internet. ⓐ 53 Meeting House Lane ⓣ 01273 770115 ⓦ www.tictoc-cafe.co.uk ⓛ 09.00–18.00 Mon–Sat, 10.00–18.00 Sun, slightly longer in summer

Love Fit Café ££ ❻ Sandwiches, pittas, paninis, salads, jacket potatoes and breakfasts can be washed down with smoothies and juices at this healthy-minded deli. Bright and funky, there's free Wi-Fi. ⓐ 14 Brighton Square ⓣ 01273 777941 ⓛ 08.00–18.00 Mon–Fri, 10.00–18.00 Sat, 10.00–17.00 Sun

Naked Tea and Coffee Co ££ ❼ Fast gaining a committed fan base, this Lanes newcomer serves an abundance of the eponymous hot drinks, along with snacks, cakes, pastries, chocolate, sandwiches and paninis. It looks on the small side from the street, but there is upstairs seating and a roof terrace. ⓐ 3 Meeting House Lane ⓛ 07.30–18.00 Mon–Wed, 07.30–22.00 Thur–Sat, 10.00–18.00 Sun

Casa Don Carlos £££ ❽ Authenticity is the watchword at this cosy, family-run Spanish eatery, where several dozen tapas dishes can be washed down with sangria or Rioja. ⓐ 5 Union Street ⓣ 01273 327177 ⓛ 10.30–23.30 daily

Moshi Moshi £££ ❽ Highly reputed conveyor-belt sushi restaurant that wins plaudits for its modern style, fresh ingredients and attention to detail. With its emphasis on sustainability and local sourcing, Moshi Moshi is understandably popular. ⓐ Opticon, Bartholomew Square ❶ 01273 719195 ⓦ www.moshibrighton.co.uk ⓛ 12.00–22.30 daily

Riddle & Finns Champagne & Oyster Bar £££ ❿ Tucked away in The Lanes, this place is not easy to find but well worth seeking out. In a lively, buzzy atmosphere, diners share high candlelit tables and choose from a delectable seafood menu, featuring

⬤ *Alfresco drinks in The Lanes*

oysters, lobster, scallops, clams and smoked salmon. The excellent food and service keep the place busy. There is no booking system but staff take your mobile number and alert you when a table is available. ⓐ 12 Meeting House Lane ① 01273 323008 ⓦ www.riddleandfinns.co.uk ① 12.00–24.00 Mon–Thur, 12.00–01.30 Fri, 09.30–01.30 Sat, 09.30–24.00 Sun

AFTER DARK

Pubs

The Cricketers ⑪ Brighton's oldest pub is as authentic and old school as it comes, though the upstairs addition has a less pubby feel. Popular and often packed, it also serves food. ⓐ 15 Black Lion Street ① 01273 329472 ① 12.00–23.00 Mon–Sat, 12.00–22.30 Sun

Clubs & bars

Casablanca Jazz Club ⑫ With separate live music and DJ rooms, the usual suspects gather at this basement venue to chill out to Latin, soul, funk, pop and Motown grooves. ⓐ 2 Middle Street ① 01273 321817 ⓦ www.casablancajazzclub.com ① currently Wed–Sat ① Admission charge on some nights

The Fish Bowl ⑬ This piscatorial-themed pub hosts regular music nights, both live bands and DJ sets. During the day the ambience is mellower, with a decent food menu. ⓐ 74 East Street ① 01273 777505 ① 11.00–23.00 Mon–Sat, 12.00–22.30 Sun

The Font ⑭ If you like the idea of making merry in a converted church, this is the place. Some great deals on drinks and simple meals, and regular entertainment, provide further reason to join the congregation. ⓐ Union Street ⓣ 01273 747727

Jam Brighton ⑮ A newcomer to Brighton's music scene, Jam's eclectic programme includes stand-up comedy, live bands, indie night, ska, funk, blues, big band, jazz, show tunes, country and western, retro and numerous other musical genres. ⓐ 9–12 Middle Street ⓣ 01273 749465 ⓛ 17.00–02.00 Sun–Thur, 17.00–03.00 Fri & Sat ⓘ Admission charge for some parts of the club

Revenge ⑯ Billing itself as the south coast's number one gay club, Revenge is a split-level venue with roof terrace and sea views. Theme nights several times a week typically go on until at least 03.00. An extensive overhaul is due to be completed in 2011. ⓐ 32–34 Old Steine ⓣ 01273 606064 ⓦ www.revenge.co.uk ⓛ schedule varies, on open nights usually 22.30 or 23.00–03.00, 04.00 or 05.00 ⓘ Admission charge

Theatres
Theatre Royal ⑰ More than two centuries old, this elegant Grade II listed building has survived 50 years on the brink of bankruptcy to become one of the UK's longest-functioning theatres. The grande dame of Brighton's theatrical scene plays host to touring productions from London's West End, as well as drama, musicals, opera, ballet and a seasonal pantomime. ⓐ New Road ⓣ 08448 717650 ⓦ www.ambassadortickets.com

The seafront

Brighton's seafront combines naff seaside fun with urban attitude, architecture and history. Yes, you've got your tarot card readers, crazy golf, inflatables vendors, family fun and a surfeit of junk food that would horrify Jamie Oliver. But there are also grand buildings (the Grand, appropriately, being one of them), funky nightclubs, sophisticated restaurants, artists' workshops and museums. Occasional pop extravaganzas (often with the involvement of the famous Brighton DJ Norman Cook, aka Fatboy Slim) lend Brighton a coolness of which Eastbourne or Blackpool could only dream. Stretching from Hove to the west, past the marina and off into charming Sussex villages to the east, Brighton's seafront bursts with _joie de vivre_, so that even the gloomiest seaside cynic will find something to enjoy.

The area covered consists of two main parallel drags: the beach itself, and the main street and promenade, which at various points is Kingsway, King's Road, Grand Junction Road and Marine Parade. The street has a wide pavement, punctuated with the odd refreshment kiosk, benches and telescopes (some of which give an audio commentary), from which you can study the piers and coastline close up. But taking the steps down to the beach itself doesn't necessarily require trudging along on the shingles – a paved walkway separates the beach proper from the many businesses and facilities that occupy the arches tucked underneath the road. Walking is the best way to take in the sights, though cycling is also popular (Brighton's coast is on a designated cycle route). If you need to get somewhere fast, several bus services also ply the coast road.

Brighton's iconic bandstand

SIGHTS & ATTRACTIONS

The beach

It may not boast the Mediterranean's pristine sands or balmy sunshine, but Brighton beach is no less loved for that – proof of this can be seen on any hot bank holiday when sun-seeking Britons descend en masse to pack the place out. Tramping along its stones, unexpectedly enormous seagulls overhead, to get your fish 'n' chip lunch is one of the quintessential English seaside experiences. Reverse bungee and crazy golf are among the cheesier entertainments, while studiedly cool youths make the most of the basketball court or the large, flat spaces for skateboarding. Few swimmers are tempted into the bracing water for most of the year, but some areas are served by lifeguards between June and mid-September.

Most of the eateries under the arches have a terrace of some sort, and an alfresco fish 'n' chip lunch is a must.

Fishing Quarter

Occupying a small area in and around the arches, this charming and atmospheric quarter consists of some pretty boats on display outside, an art gallery and a museum. Though the Fishing Quarter has the feel of a tourist zone rather than of an authentic piscatorial area, boats are indeed repaired and restored on site. ⓐ On beach, between the two piers

The Grand

Lording it over Brighton's seafront, the Grand more than lives up to its proud name (though its five-star status has lapsed owing to a lack of investment). The hotel was built on the site of a former battery house in 1864 to cater to the well-heeled holidaymakers flocking to the newly fashionable Brighton. Bright and eye-catching, the building's Italian-inspired Victorian design has made it one of Brighton's most recognisable landmarks. It found further, though more sobering, fame as the target of an infamous terrorist attack (see box on page 25).

Brighton Pier

Gloriously tacky it may be, and it certainly divides the locals, but Brighton's iconic pier is a temple to frivolous pleasure that no visitor should miss. That you are stepping into a different zone is obvious from the food kiosks that form a crescent at the entrance. Doughnuts, sweets, pancakes, ice cream and fish and chips provide edible proof that the UK's recent health drive stops where the dry land ends. Once you're on the pier, it's all about gratification. Along its length are benches – helpfully covered to protect the occupants from wind and rain – and, more optimistically, deckchairs. The first major feature you come to is the Palace of Fun, the main amusement arcade. Further on you will come to a restaurant and a couple of pubs, before a smaller amusements arcade and then the fairground, where the mini log flume Wild River, Roller coaster, Booster, Waltzer and Beat the Bull bucking bronco await to slide, shake and spin you into submission. If you prefer to remain more static, there's also Dolphin Derby and an old-school Helter Skelter. Seaside stalwarts like fortune-tellers, old-fashioned photos, artists, jellied eels, rock and candyfloss complete the picture. ⓐ Madeira Drive

❶ 01273 609361 ⓦ www.brightonpier.co.uk
🕙 09.00–24.00 daily (summer); 10.00–24.00 daily (winter)

Sea Life Centre

Fishy family fun at what is billed as the oldest operating
aquarium in the world. Housed in a Victorian building, the
Sea Life Centre is home to over 150 aquatic species. Highlights
include two giant turtles and everybody's favourite underwater
villain, the shark. A glass-bottomed boat, which takes visitors
back and forth as fish encircle it, is a recent addition. ❸ Madeira
Drive ❶ 0871 423 2110 ⓦ www.sealife.co.uk 🕙 10.00–18.00 daily
Easter–Sept, 10.00–17.00 daily Sept–Easter ❶ Admission charge

🔺 *Brighton Pier at dusk*

Volk's Electric Railway

Initially intended as a temporary summer attraction, Magnus Volk's narrow-gauge track, work on which started in the 1880s, is today the world's oldest operating electric railway. Trains run between Brighton Pier and the marina, a distance of 2 km (1¼ miles). The slow speed is not thrilling, but the train provides a relaxing and leisurely way to take in the scenery.

ⓐ 285 Madeira Drive ❶ 01273 292718
ⓦ www.volkselectricrailway.co.uk ❶ 10.00–17.00 Mon–Fri, 10.00–18.00 Sat & Sun Easter–mid-Sept, closed rest of the year
❶ Admission charge

West Pier

Looking rather forlorn alongside its bustling, fully lit neighbour, West Pier is in fact one of only two Grade I listed piers in Britain. Completed in 1866, the pier housed a concert hall in its glory days, but history wasn't kind. Damaged in World War II, the pier fell into disrepair and was closed in 1975. Then in 2002 it partially collapsed and went up in flames a year later. Plans are afoot to renovate it and install the *i360*, or Brighton Eye, a 183-m (600-ft) observation tower, by 2011.

CULTURAL ATTRACTIONS

Fishing Museum and Gallery

Far from a dusty collection of unremarkable nautical scenes, as some might expect from such a venue, the gallery hosts a rotating programme of exhibitions that features everything from drawings, cartoons and photographs to 2D and 3D mixed media. In the museum are further large fishing vessels (an 8 m/27 ft clinker-built punt boat is the star exhibit), historic photos, memorabilia, videos and an old bell; some special effects are even employed. A friendly volunteer is usually on hand to answer questions. ⓐ On beach, between the two piers ⓦ www.brightonfishingmuseum.org.uk ⓛ 10.00–17.00 daily Gallery ⓛ 11.00–17.00 daily (summer)

Old Penny Arcade Museum

Day-trippers to Brighton have been popping coins into colourful boxes since the Victorian era, and this small museum showcases the development of the seaside staple of slot machines. Your modern currency buys you old pennies which can be inserted into the machines; given their state of superannuation, do not be surprised if they are not all in working order. Distorting mirrors add to the fairground fun. ⓐ King's Road Arches, between the two piers ⓣ 01273 608620 ⓛ 12.00–18.00 daily (Easter–Sept); sunny weekends (winter)

TAKING A BREAK

Horatio's £ ⑱ Another archetypal pub, with high stools, round tables, two beer gardens and sport on the big screen. Children are permitted until 20.00. ⓐ End of Brighton Pier, near funfair ⓣ 01273 609361 ⓛ 12.00–18.00, 19.00–late daily (summer), 12.00–18.00, 19.00–late Sat & Sun, closed weekdays (winter)

Victoria's Bar £ ⑲ One of two traditional British boozers on Brighton Pier, Victoria's Bar's USP is the 'most interesting ceiling

you've ever seen'; indeed, look up and you'll see a pram, boat and drum among other suspended items. As well as the alcohol, they serve basket meals, tea, coffee and muffins, and punters can also bring their own food in. Live sport is broadcast.
ⓐ Brighton Pier ☎ 01273 609361 🕐 09.00–22.00 daily (summer), 10.00–18.00 or 19.00 daily (winter)

World Famous Pump Room £ ⓴ Fiercely proud of the historic sign announcing the café, this is a friendly little outfit serving locally sourced snacks which can be consumed at outside tables.
ⓐ 121–122 King's Road Arches, by sand pit ☎ 01273 203139 🕐 09.00–21.00 daily

Lodestar Café ££ ㉑ A relative newcomer to the seafront scene, Lodestar's stock in trade is typical café fare: baguettes, sandwiches, salads and soup, with a range of cakes and cookies to round it off. ⓐ 163 King's Road Arches ☎ 01273 252516
ⓦ www.lodestarcafe.co.uk 🕐 10.00–18.00 daily

Moo Moos ££ ㉒ Bright and cheerful, this bovine-themed outlet's main trade is in milkshakes, available in hundreds of flavours, but the sweet-toothed can also pick up biscuits, cakes and sweets. ⓐ Brighton Pier 🕐 Pier hours (see pages 59–60)

Palm Court Restaurant ££ ㉓ Thoroughly decent pier eatery, serving standard British fare such as bangers and mash and steak and kidney pie as well as location-appropriate dishes such as fish and chips. The mellow, old-fashioned music and photos of Brighton in days gone by set a traditional tone,

but the bright blue-and-white décor is modern and inviting.
🅐 Brighton Pier 📞 01273 609361 🕒 11.30–20.00 or 21.00 Mon–Fri,
11.30–21.00 or 22.00 (summer), 11.30–17.00 Mon–Fri, 11.30–20.00
Sat & Sun (winter)

◓ *The interior of the Brighton Fishing Museum*

Regency Restaurant ££ ㉔ Serving up great-value seafood since 1965, the Regency is as classy as its name suggests. Service is fast and the food good, and the place has fully earned its plaudits from critics and famous fans. ⓐ 131 King's Road ⓣ 01273 325014 ⓦ www.theregencyrestaurant.co.uk ⓛ 08.00–23.00 daily

Due South £££ ㉕ Big on presentation, sustainability and quality, top-notch Due South has been raising the bar for Brighton restaurants in the seven years of its existence. The menu, which changes monthly, draws on local ingredients to provide a wealth of superb seafood and unexpected highlights such as rabbit terrine – rustled up in full view in the glass kitchen. ⓐ 139 King's Road Arches ⓣ 01273 821218 ⓦ www.duesouth.co.uk ⓛ 12.00–15.30, 18.00–22.00 daily (summer), 12.00–15.30, 18.00–22.00 Wed–Sat & Mon, 12.00–15.30 Sun closed Tues (winter)

AFTER DARK

Coalition ㉖ Music, club nights, comedy and entertainment all hold court at this stylish venue. ⓐ 171 King's Road Arches ⓣ 01273 726858 ⓦ www.brightoncoalition.co.uk ⓛ Café 11.00–21.00 daily; club usually 22.30–04.00 Thur–Tues, closed Wed

Funky Buddha Lounge ㉗ Scruffs can forget it at this cosy club, purveyor of soul, funk, R&B, hip-hop, house and disco late into the night. ⓐ 169–170 King's Road Arches ⓣ 01273 725541 ⓛ usually 23.00–late on open nights, days vary

Glitterball ❷❽ It couldn't be a proper seaside experience without karaoke, even though the opening hours are somewhat limited. ⓐ Brighton Pier, next to Horatio's ❶ 01273 609361 ⓦ www.theglitterballbar.co.uk ❸ 14.00–23.00 Sat, closed Sun–Mon

Honey Club ❷❾ Five-room seafront club and terrace pumping out funky house, R&B, salsa, indie and more to a dressy, serious crowd. ⓐ 214 King's Road Arches ❶ 01273 202807, 07000 446639 ⓦ www.thehoneyclub.co.uk ❸ Café 11.00–between 18.00 and 22.00 daily (Easter–Oct); club 23.00–03.00 Tues, Thur, Sun, 23.00–04.00 Fri, 23.00–05.00 Sat (year round)

Volk's Bar & Club ❸⓿ With snacks and chill-out music during the day in season, at night the eclectic musical menu spans the genres, taking in reggae and dancehall, techno, house, funk, drum n bass, breaks, dubstep and party. Housed in a century-old colonnade, the name is a nod to the railway engineer. ⓐ 3 Madeira Drive ❶ 01273 682828 ⓦ www.volksclub.co.uk ❸ Café 11.00 daily (Apr–Oct), club nights 22.00 or 23.00– between 04.00 and 08.00 days vary (year round)

Around and north of Brighton Station

If your trip is brief, you might not have time for much beyond the very heart of the town and the seafront. However, some of Brighton's lesser-known highlights lie to the north of the main action, and are included in this section. The area starts from **North Laine**, a district often confused with – or overlooked in favour of – The Lanes. But this bohemian quarter has a quite different vibe from its more famous, touristy counterpart. Moving north is the station zone, with some attractions close by. Further north still, by now about 1.6 km (1 mile) from the sea, are the **Booth Museum of Natural History**, **Preston Park** and **Manor**, the northern limit of the territory covered here.

SIGHTS & ATTRACTIONS

Duke of York's Picturehouse
Britain's longest-operating cinema still looks much as it did when it first opened, a full century ago. The Grade II listed building, which is also one of the oldest cinemas in the world, is Edwardian Baroque in style. The elegant façade is somewhat overshadowed by the large pair of model legs – in black and white tights and high heels, and doing the cancan – on the roof. Though incongruous, overall they add to the charm. ⓐ Preston Circus ⓘ 0871 704 2056 ⓦ www.picturehouses.co.uk

North Laine
A mecca for alternative types, North Laine is something of a Camden-on-Sea. Bursting with rebellious spirit, it's a great place

to wander and imbibe Brighton's anarchic vibe. One of North Laine's main attractions, comedy club Komedia, occupies a site that was formerly a supermarket. In another revealing retail detail, the first branch of The Body Shop was also established here. Between The Lanes and Brighton Station

Preston Park

It may not be a tourist must-see, but if the weather is fine and you have the time, Preston Park is an agreeable place for a stroll or a picnic. Features include the rose gardens, bowling greens and pond; you might also find some football going on. It's all very English, and foreign visitors in particular will get something out of the experience. Just north of the park is St Peter's, a 13th-century chapel with wall paintings of the murder of St Thomas à Becket in Canterbury Cathedral, and a rare Tudor tomb. (Preston Drove 07762 484814 11.00–15.00 daily (winter); longer hours in summer). To the west, the other side of the main road, is The Rockery, the UK's largest municipal rock garden. Occupying the side of a railway embankment, it's a delightful spot, with meandering pathways, streams, charming bridges and stepping stones. Between Preston Road and Preston Park Avenue Train: Preston Park, bus: 5, 5A, 17, 40, 40X, 88, 273

Preston Manor

This four-storey manor house has the distinction of being dubbed Britain's most haunted house. The original 13th-century structure is sadly no more; its replacement began life in the 1730s but an Edwardian atmosphere now prevails. The house also serves as a revealing embodiment of the British class system, the servants' quarters in sharp juxtaposition to the plush nursery. ⓐ Preston Drove ⓣ 03000 290900 ⓦ www.brighton-hove-rpml.org.uk ⓛ 10.15–16.15 Tues–Sat, escorted visits at 14.15, 15.15, 16.15 Sun, closed Mon (Apr–Sept); closed rest of year ⓝ Train: Preston Park; Bus: 5, 5A, 59, 86, 87, 273 ⓘ Admission charge. Gardens ⓛ open all year

St Bartholomew's Church

One of Europe's tallest brick churches, lofty St Bartholomew's looms impressively high – 44 m (144 ft) including the gilt cross – over the area around Brighton Station. The Grade I listed

▲ *The kitchen at Preston Manor*

neo-Gothic building opened in 1874. ⓐ Ann Street
ⓣ 01273 620491 ⓦ www.stbartholomewsbrighton.org.uk
ⓛ 10.00–13.00, 14.00–16.30 Mon–Sat, for services on Sun

St Peter's Church

Cited as an exemplar of the pre-Victorian Gothic Revival
style, Grade II-listed St Peter's dates from the 1820s. Ornate
and attractive, highlights include the stained-glass windows
and sizeable pipe organ. ⓐ York Place ⓣ 01273 698182
ⓦ www.stpetersbrighton.org ⓛ office 09.30–17.30 Mon–Thur,
closed Fri–Sun

⬥ *The massive brick tower of St Bartholomew's*

ST BARTHOLOMEW'S CHURCH

Although now almost universally considered a plus point for Brighton, St Bartholomew's Church was not always so revered. A suspicion of Catholic proclivities already hung around the Reverend Arthur Wagner, who was responsible for the building's design. At a town council meeting in 1893 it was revealed that the church was 60 cm (2 ft) taller than the height specified in the approved plan. Wagner was too wealthy for the statutory fine for the discrepancy to be worth imposing on him, but the town councillors took the opportunity to excoriate the church, pronouncing it 'a cheese warehouse', 'a Noah's Ark in brick', 'a monster excrescence', 'a brick parallelogram', 'a huge barn', 'uselessly large, painfully ugly and sadly out of place', and 'Wagner's folly'.

CULTURE

Booth Museum of Natural History

The ambitious mission of the ornithologist Edward Booth was to capture one specimen of every species of British bird. The Victorian display method – environmental diorama – gives the place an old-fashioned feel, but also confers the eccentricity that memorable museums often have. ⓐ 194 Dyke Road ⓣ 03000 290900 ⓦ www.brighton.virtualmuseum.info ⓛ 10.00–17.00 Mon–Wed, Fri & Sat, 14.00–17.00 Sun, closed Thur ⓝ Bus: 27, 27A

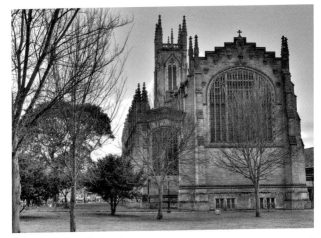

🔾 *Imposing St Peter's Church*

Brighton Toy and Model Museum

Prepare to immerse yourself in nostalgia. The Smurfs, Meccano, Matchbox cars and Pelham Puppets are among the staggering 10,000 toys on display in the museum, which is tucked away in the railway arches. Children will be engrossed, as will the young at heart. ⓐ 52–55 Trafalgar Street ⓣ 01273 749494 ⓦ www.brightontoymuseum.co.uk ⓛ 10.00–17.00 Tues–Fri, 11.00–17.00 Sat, closed Sun & Mon ⓘ Admission charge

RETAIL THERAPY

Countercultural North Laine offers a quirky and enticing mix of shops. Second-hand records, vintage clothes, vegetarian shoes (sic), arty knick-knacks, foreign finds and holistic paraphernalia are the typical merchandise here, which draws in the hippie or student shopper. Even if none of this is your bag, the efforts made by the independent stores to prettify and individualise their premises make a refreshing change from the standard high-street-y surrounds. North Laine is worth a wander even if you're not buying.

In tune with its bohemian character, North Laine is also home to a weekly flea market. Wares range from antiques and homewares to fruit and veg. ⓐ Upper Gardner Street ⓦ www.brightonstreetmarket.co.uk ⓛ from 09.00 Sat

Beyond Retro

They say 'beyond retro' and they mean it: this Swedish vintage boutique has clobber up to a century old, sourced by fashion experts who scour the globe for sartorial gems. ⓐ 42 Vine Street ⓣ 01273 671937 ⓦ www.beyondretro.com ⓛ 10.00–18.00 Mon–Wed, Fri & Sat, 10.00–20.00 Thur, 11.00–17.00 Sun

Fair

North Laine's ethos is perfectly encapsulated in this fair-trade boutique. On sale within are fashion, accessories, toiletries, homewares and gifts, with the ethical keywords 'organic', 'natural' and 'handmade'. The store funnels some of its takings into more than 50 charitable projects, alleviating the guilt of any splurge. It also hosts regular events. ⓐ 21 Queen's Road ⓣ 01273 723215 ⓦ www.thefairshop.co.uk ⓛ 10.00–18.00 Mon–Wed, Fri & Sat, 10.00–19.00 Thur, 11.00–17.30 Sun, closed bank holidays

Guttersnipe Clothing

Its stated target demographic of 'street urchins, punks, mods, spivs, lovers and cheeky monkeys' should convey a flavour of what this anarchic shop is all about. ⓐ 94A Gloucester Road ⓣ 01273 670555 ⓦ guttersnipesclothing.co.uk ⓛ 10.30–17.30 Mon, Wed–Fri, 10.00–17.30 Sat, 11.00–16.00 Sun, closed Tues

The Wax Factor

Operating since the 1980s, the Wax Factor (the absolute antithesis of the TV talent show whose name it calls to mind) brims with vinyl, CDs, DVDs, cassettes (remember them?) and alternative books. The genres covered range from rock to reggae and soul to soundtracks. The affiliated Rock Ola Café at No 29 Tidy Street has a food menu and a free jukebox. ⓐ 24 Trafalgar Street ⓣ 01273 673744 ⓦ www.thewaxfactor.com ⓛ 10.15–17.30 Mon–Fri, 9.45–17.30 Sat, closed Sun

TAKING A BREAK

Bystander Café £ ③① Recently spruced up, Bystander's menu complements some Italian standards with burgers, veggie burgers, baked potatoes and omelettes. There's Wi-Fi and some outside tables. ⓐ 1 Terminus Road ⓣ 01273 329364 ⓛ 08.00–24.00 daily

Divalls Café £ ③② Cheerfully decorated in red and white and with a television advertising station arrivals and departures, cosy Divalls has comfortable seats by the window, excellent coffee and delicious home-made cookies among the hot and cold fare. It also has free Wi-Fi. ⓐ 3 Terminus Road ⓣ 07832 104455 ⓦ www.divalls.co.uk ⓛ 06.30–22.00 daily

Laine Deli £ ③ Billing itself as the 'brightest, happiest coffee shop and delicatessen in Brighton', the Laine Deli serves sandwiches, bagels and ciabattas as well as soup, pasties and quiches, all with a smile. If it's warm, head for the patio. ⓐ 31 Trafalgar Street ⓣ 01273 686665 ⓦ www.thelainedeli.co.uk ⓛ 08.00–16.00 Mon–Fri, 09.30–15.30 Sat, closed Sun

Toast in Brighton £ ③ This homely, friendly sandwich and espresso bar has an extensive and tempting sandwich and toastie menu, and also serves breakfast, salads, soups and smoothies. It's cosy, with just one table inside, a few outside and a leather armchair. ⓐ 38 Trafalgar Street ⓣ 01273 626888 ⓛ 07.30–15.30 Mon–Fri, closed Sat & Sun

Nia ££ ③ By day it's a café, but after 18.00 Nia goes into restaurant mode, with a bold Mediterranean-inspired menu with meat, fish and veggie options. Vibrant, ethical and friendly. ⓐ 87–88 Trafalgar Street ⓣ 01273 671371 ⓦ www.nia-brighton.co.uk ⓛ 09.00–22.00 Mon–Sat, 09.00–17.00 Sun

Painting Pottery Café ££ ③ Arty, crafty fun for creative types, from beginners to pottery veterans. ⓐ 31 North Road ⓣ 01273 628952 ⓦ www.paintingpotterycafe.co.uk ⓛ 11.00–18.30 or 19.00 Tues, Wed, Fri & Sat, 11.00–22.00 Thur, bookings only Sun, closed Mon

TFI Lunch ££ ③ Sister outlet to The Lanes branch, serving the same array of tempting light lunches and breakfast menu.
ⓐ 56 Queen's Road ① 01273 720017 ⓦ www.tfilunch.com
① 07.00–15.00 Mon–Fri, closed Sat & Sun

Seven Dials £££ ③ What was once a branch of Lloyds Bank has been reborn as a confident and stylish family-owned restaurant. The contemporary European and British menu is regularly updated and uses fresh, seasonal ingredients.
ⓐ 1 Buckingham Place ① 01273 885555
ⓦ www.sevendialsrestaurant.co.uk ① 12.00–22.00 Mon–Fri, 12.00–23.30 Sat, 10.00–16.00 Sun

AFTER DARK

Cinemas
Duke of York's Picturehouse ③ Britain's oldest continuously operating purpose-built cinema is best known today as an art-house venue. It shows up to five features a day, and the varied programme also includes classic film, documentaries, children's productions and the latest releases. The cinema hosts special events, such as fancy-dress premieres, all-night movie marathons and late-night cult films. ⓐ Preston Circus
① 0871 704 2056 ⓦ www.picturehouses.co.uk

Comedy clubs
Komedia ④ Known primarily as a comedy club – as the name suggests – this Brighton institution also stages music, cabaret, theatre, club nights and children's events. Many of stand-up's

◔ *The Duke of York's Picturehouse*

elite, including Graham Norton, Johnny Vegas, Al Murray, Jenny Éclair and Alistair McGowan, played Komedia in their salad days. ⓐ 44 Gardner Street ⓣ 01273 647100 ⓦ www.komedia.co.uk

Pubs

Three Jolly Butchers ⓫ Lively and friendly pub serving popular
pub grub. The attached sandwich shop (ⓛ 08.00–15.00 Mon–Fri, closed Sat & Sun) is also highly thought of. The décor is modern while retaining some more rustic elements. Happy hour and open-mic night add to the mix. ⓐ 59 North Road ⓣ 01273 608571 ⓛ 12.00–24.00 Sun–Thur, 12.00–02.00 Fri & Sat

The Park View ⓬ Ideally placed to precede or round off a trip
to Preston Park, this family-friendly venue does a gastropub menu and hosts tai chi, salsa and a weekly quiz. There's an attractive beer garden and a range of ales for those who take their beer seriously. ⓐ 71 Preston Drove ⓣ 01273 541663 ⓦ theparkviewbrighton.co.uk ⓛ 12.00–23.30 Mon–Thur, 12.00–24.00 Fri, 10.00–24.00 Sat, 10.00–23.30 Sun ⓥ Bus: 5B, 55, 88

▶ *The Seven Sisters at Birling Gap*

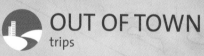

OUT OF TOWN
trips

Lewes

With its pastoral setting and easy historic air, the charming county town Lewes (pronounced Lewis) provides a perfect counterpoint to the urban energy of Brighton. Nestled in a gap in the South Downs, it's a place for pottering, leisurely sightseeing and afternoon tea. Georgian town houses, country cottages, flinty churches and old-fashioned independent businesses (among the inevitable high-street ubiquities) complement several historic sites and pretty wandering areas like **Keere Street** and **Cliffe Bridge**, to which it is well worth devoting at least half a day.

GETTING THERE

Several bus routes run frequently between Brighton and Lewes, taking around half an hour. Equally convenient train services take half that. The town is an easy drive from Brighton, via the A270 and A27; if you don't hit traffic you can be there in under 20 minutes.

SIGHTS & ATTRACTIONS

Anne of Cleves House

The name is rather a misnomer, as Henry VIII's fourth wife never in fact visited this 15th-century timber-framed house, part of her post-annulment payoff from the multi-marrying king (a better deal than others got!). The best room is the bedroom, which has period costumes to try on before the mirror, and pots containing

olden-day smells (rose, lavender, urine and horse and stables).
ⓐ 52 High Street **ⓣ** 01273 474610 **ⓦ** www.sussexpast.co.uk
ⓛ 10.00–17.00 Tues–Thur, 11.00–17.00 Sun, Mon & bank holidays
Mar–Oct, closed Nov–Feb **ⓘ** Admission charge; combined ticket
with Lewes Castle

Lewes Castle

As well as its impressive historic pedigree, this well-preserved
Norman fortress offers interactive jinks for children and
extraordinary views – provided you're not averse to climbing.
Visitors will enjoy squeezing into alcoves, trying on further
period costumes, aiming a crossbow and building a castle wall.
The views from the castle apex are glorious, but getting to that
vantage point means negotiating an extremely narrow and
nerve-racking spiral staircase. A small museum and audiovisual
history show complete the line-up. **ⓐ** 169 High Street

▲ Lewes Castle

GUNPOWDER, TREASON AND PLOT FIRE UP LEWES

More than any other town, Lewes has embraced Guy Fawkes' Day, which commemorates the failed attempt by a band of Catholic conspirators to blow up the Houses of Parliament on 5 November 1605. The event was marked only sporadically by locals until the 1820s, when gangs of so-called Bonfire Boys started a tradition of setting off random fireworks, lighting pyres and rolling barrels of tar through the streets. The annual fracas got so raucous that in the 1840s London police were drafted in to maintain order. The bedlam was soon shaped into a more orderly celebration, which has become the UK's largest Guy Fawkes' Day event. Today, it takes the form of torch-lit costumed parades by organised bonfire societies. Proceedings culminate in the burning of effigies, with targets in recent years including popular villains from politicians and bankers to international terrorists.

🛈 01273 486290 🕐 10.00–17.30 Tues–Sat, 11.00–17.30 Sun, Mon and bank holidays ❶ Admission charge; combined ticket with Anne of Cleves House

Southover Grange

Though the striking 16th-century house itself is not open to visitors, the grounds are well worth a wander, both for their aesthetic value and Elizabethan vestiges. Beautifully arranged flowerbeds, pretty water features and an atmosphere of refined tranquillity make the gardens one of Lewes's jewels. A terrace operates daily in summer from 09.00–17.00 ⓐ Southover High Street, Lewes ⓛ dawn–dusk daily

TAKING A BREAK

Fillers £ Amiable café serving a selection of sandwiches, baguettes and breakfast options. ⓐ 19–21 Market Street ⓣ 01273 477042 ⓛ 07.00–17.00 Mon–Fri, 08.00–16.00 Sat, closed Sun

Chaula's Indian Café Restaurant ££ A little piece of India in Sussex, this convivial eatery purveys traditional vegetarian Gujarati cuisine along with some meat and fish curries. ⓐ 6 Eastgate Street ⓣ 01273 476707 ⓦ www.chaulas.co.uk ⓛ 10.00–15.00, 17.00–23.00 Mon–Thur, 11.00–23.00 Fri & Sat, closed Sun & bank holidays

Pelham House ££ The 16th-century garden room provides the historic dining environs at Pelham House. Highlights include lamb gigot steak, and pan-fried scallops, sage and lemon. ⓐ St Andrews Lane ⓣ 01273 488600 ⓦ www.pelhamhouse.com ⓛ lunch from 12.00 daily, dinner from 18.30 daily

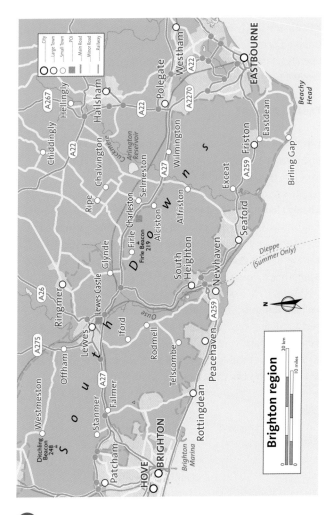

Brighton region

East along the coast

From Brighton's built-up metropolitanism it is but a brief remove to the rolling hills of the South Downs, which exemplify England's fabled green and pleasant land. Georgian terraces and hip nightclubs rapidly give way to bucolic scenes of gambolling lambs and quaint tea rooms. The area east of the city affords plenty of opportunity for unhurried constitutionals, gentle sightseeing and pub lunching.

GETTING THERE

Brighton's bus network serves the villages to the east of the town, and if you only plan to visit one or two places public transport should suffice. The tourist office (see page 93) can even help with planning, issuing leaflets that link up various walks and sights with the relevant bus route. However, there can be protracted gaps between services, and if you want to cover several points in the vicinity in a more convenient way, car is the way to do it.

SIGHTS & ATTRACTIONS

Alfriston

After the sleepiness of many other villages in the area, touristy Alfriston (pronounced All-friston) comes as quite a shock. Tea rooms and souvenir shops proliferate along the High Street, which doesn't quite throng with holidaymakers and day-trippers, but is certainly on the busy side by South Downs

standards. The reason is evident: Alfriston is almost ridiculously pretty. The largely 14th-century St Andrew's parish church, Alfriston Clergy House and Star Inn are just the most high profile of the village's delightful buildings. Its attributes are said to have inspired the hymn *Morning has Broken*.

Birling Gap

The coastal hamlet on the chalk cliffs known as the Seven Sisters has a certain poignancy as it is threatened by erosion: some of its fishing cottages have already perished and many of the remaining ones are unoccupied. The clean beach is popular with naturists. ⓐ Birling Gap Road, East Dean

Charleston

The rural outpost of the Bloomsbury Set, the circle of writers, artists and thinkers that included sisters Virginia Woolf and

⬥ *Alfriston parish church*

Vanessa Bell, Charleston also offers a phenomenal art collection, including works by Picasso and Renoir. In May the Charleston Festival attracts the cream of the literary crop. ⓐ Between Firle and Selmeston, signposted off the A27 ❶ 01323 811265 ⓦ www.charleston.org.uk ⓛ 13.00–18.00 Wed–Sat, 13.00–17.30 Sun & bank holiday Mon, closed Mon & Tues Apr–Jun, Sept & Oct, 12.00–18.00 Wed–Sat, 13.00–17.30 Sun & bank holiday Mon July & Aug, closed Nov–Feb ❶ Admission charge

Exceat

Pronounced 'Exy-at', the ancient village is sadly no more. However, very pleasant rural walks can be done from the car park by the Golden Galleon pub. ⓐ On the A259, east of the River Cuckmere

Long Man of Wilmington

This chalk figure, nearly 70 m (230 ft) tall, is cut into the hillside, and appears in proportion when viewed from the ground below. It probably dates back to the 16th or 17th century. In 1874 the outline was marked with yellow bricks by a reverend, causing some to complain that this distorted the feet and prudishly did away with the Long Man's genitals. ⓐ Wilmington, off the A27

Rodmell

Simply passing through Rodmell is a pleasure in itself. But the significance of this charming village lies mainly in its being the location of Monk's House, the 18th-century weatherboarded cottage that served as Virginia Woolf's country retreat. The troubled genius wrote many of her novels in the wooden garden

lodge here; she also drowned herself in the nearby River Ouse.
Monk's House ⓐ Rodmell ⓣ 01323 870001 ⓛ 14.00–17.30 Wed &
Sat May–Oct ⓘ Admission charge

TAKING A BREAK

Abergavenny Arms ££ Traditional English country pub with
an upmarket food menu and a pleasant garden. ⓐ Rodmell
ⓣ 01273 472416 ⓦ www.abergavennyarms.com ⓛ 11.00–23.00
Mon–Thur, Sat, 10.00–23.00 Fri, 12.00–22.00 Sun

Moonrakers £££ With a fascinating smuggling history alluded
to in its name, Moonrakers serves a temptingly ambitious
menu – highlights include slow-cooked partridge and duck
gizzards – in two beamed dining rooms. ⓐ High Street, Alfriston
ⓣ 01323 871199 ⓦ www.moonrakersrestaurant.co.uk
ⓛ 12.00–15.00, 18.00–24.00 Wed–Sat, 12.00–17.00 Sun, closed
Mon & Tues

ⓞ *An old sign in Lewes*

30 MILES
FROM THE STANDARD
IN CORNHILL.
49 TO WESTMINSTER BRIDGE
8 MILES TO BRIGHTHELMST NW

PRACTICAL
information

Directory

GETTING THERE

Regular rail services run between Brighton and several London stations, including Victoria and London Bridge, taking less than an hour. Train services also link Brighton with the other major south-coast towns Hastings, Portsmouth and Southampton. Advance fares from London start at less than £10; it's almost always more expensive to just turn up and buy your ticket on the spot. Coaches from London take two hours and advance fares can be as low as £2.

It's not possible to fly into the immediate vicinity of Brighton – unless you own your own plane – but Gatwick Airport is conveniently located. If you're driving from London, the main route is the A23. From the very centre of town, it's about an hour and a half, though times can vary wildly according to traffic.

Many people are aware that air travel emits CO_2, which contributes to climate change. You may be interested in the possibility of lessening the environmental impact of your flight through the charity **Climate Care** (Ⓦ www.jpmorganclimatecare.com), which offsets your CO_2 by funding environmental projects around the world.

HEALTH, SAFETY & CRIME

Although Brighton's crime rates are slightly higher than the UK average, it is not a particularly dangerous town in which to spend time. Like any British town with a concentration of bars and nightclubs, at 'chucking-out time' drunken club-goers can loiter in the streets, and the late-night atmosphere can be somewhat intimidating, although trouble seldom spreads to innocent passers-by.

Brighton's reputation as a party destination means younger people may occasionally be approached by drug dealers at night, but a firm 'no' should put an end to the situation.

Safety risks can be minimised by avoiding the vicinity of clubs and bars late at night. All standard urban safety precautions – keeping wallets in secured bags or pockets, not advertising valuables, avoiding deserted areas after dark – apply. Lewes and the villages mentioned in the 'out of town' section are just about as crime free as it gets in England.

Though for most of the year the concept of sunburn or heatstroke in Brighton would be regarded as an ironic joke, the wave of euphoria that greets any hot weekend can lead people to throw caution to the wind and forget precautions: sunscreen, covering up during the hottest hours and drinking fluids. The weather largely precludes night-swimming, but drunken carousers have perished after taking to the water, which is never advisable in those conditions. So-called tombstoning, a perilous craze where people hurl themselves from piers, bridges or cliffs into water below, is exceptionally risky.

If you find yourself in need of emergency dental treatment, call 0300 1000 899 and the operator will make you an appointment at one of the city's surgeries.

In a health emergency, dial 999 or 112. An accident and emergency department can be found at the Royal Sussex County Hospital ⓐ Eastern Road ⓣ 01273 696955. For non-urgent medical help, the best recourse is NHS Direct ⓣ 0845 4647 ⓦ www.nhsdirect.nhs.uk

OPENING HOURS

Brighton's attractions tend to come to life between 09.00 and 10.00 and close their doors around 17.00 or 18.00. Smaller or quieter places may operate reduced hours, sometimes afternoons only. If there is a closed day, it is likely to be Monday, but this is not a hard-and-fast rule. Shops tend to open 09.00–18.00, perhaps later on Saturday and with occasional late-night shopping on Thursday running through until about 20.00. By law stores can only open for six hours on Sunday, usually 11.00–17.00. Local shops selling essentials are often open longer.

TOILETS

Brighton's public toilets are generally of a decent standard; the council website features a useful map of their locations. All tourist attractions should have washrooms, and you can often use the facilities at eateries and hotels if caught short, either discreetly or with staff permission, if nothing else is available.

CHILDREN

Brighton is an excellent place to bring young visitors. The beach and pier have endless entertainments for children. On the seafront there are activities like crazy golf and reverse bungee, as well as all the simple rewards afforded by beach and sea. Only the staple seaside pastime of building a sandcastle is missing, owing to the lack of sand. Many of the attractions included in this guide – the Sea Life Centre, Brighton Toy and Model Museum, the Old Penny Arcade Museum – will delight young children; slightly older ones might also enjoy the Royal Pavilion. If the weather is warm, Preston Park's Rockery can make a change from the beach.

TRAVELLERS WITH DISABILITIES

Except where logistics prohibit it, many of Brighton's attractions and businesses have made an effort to make their premises wheelchair-friendly. Brighton Pier, for example, is highly popular with visitors with limited mobility, and has a separate disabled toilet. The Brighton Visitor Information Centre (see below) is an excellent source of information for travellers with disabilities, listing accessible sights, hotels and restaurants with downloadable factsheets on its website, also available in large print, Braille or audio tape.

FURTHER INFORMATION

Brighton has a helpful tourist office and gift shop by the Royal Pavilion ⓐ 4–5 Pavilion Buildings ⓣ 0300 300 0088 ⓦ www.visitbrighton.com ⓛ 09.30–17.15 daily (summer); 10.00–17.00 daily (winter). There is a wealth of useful information on the town's official tourist website, as is there on the Brighton & Hove City Council site (ⓦ www.brighton-hove.gov.uk).

BACKGROUND READING

The classic Brighton novel is of course Graham Greene's *Brighton Rock*, although this dark underworld tale of murder and sociopathy is hardly a flattering tribute. More uplifting is *The Brighton Book*, an anthology of essays, poetry, pictures and more from contributors including Louis de Bernières, Jeanette Winterson and Nigella Lawson. Outspoken writer Julie Burchill, a long-time local resident, has also centred much of her prolific output on her adoptive city.

A

Abba 48
Abergavenny Arms 88
accommodation 22–5
airports 32, 90
Alfriston 85–6
amusement arcades 59
Angel Food Bakery 51
Anne of Cleves House
  80–81
annual events 8–9
Antique House, The 49
Artists' Open House 12
Artist Quarter 12
arts *see* culture
attractions
  around and north of
    Brighton Station 67–70
  city centre 45–7
  east along the coast 85–8
  free 30
  Lewes 80–3
  seafront 58–61
  top 26–7
  wet weather 31

B

B&B 22
Baggies Backpackers 22
beach 26, 58
Beyond Retro 72–3
Birling Gap 86
Booth Museum of Natural
  History 71
Brighton Big Beach
  Boutique 18
Brighton Dome 45
Brighton Eye 61
Brighton Festival & Fringe
  8–9, 27
Brighton Live 9
Brighton Marina 15
Brighton Museum & Art
  Gallery 12, 27, 48–9
Brighton Pier 26, 59–60
Brighton Pride 9
Brighton Racecourse 21
Brighton Toy and Model
  Museum 72
Burning the Clocks 9
buses 38
Bystander Café 74

C

cafés 52, 63, 74–5, 83
camping and caravanning
  23
car hire 40
Casa Don Carlos 52
Casablanca Jazz Club 54
Charleston 86–7
Chaula's Indian Café
  Restaurant 83
children 92
Choccywoccydoodah 50
churches and chapels 68,
  69–70
Churchill Square Shopping
  Centre 15, 49
cinemas 18, 67, 76
city areas 42
  around and north of
    Brighton Station 67–78
  city centre 44–56
  seafront 57–66
city centre 44–56
climate 8
Climate Care 90
Clock Tower 45–6
clubs and performance
  venues 55–6, 65–6, 76
coaches 33, 90
Coalition 65
comedy venues 56, 65, 76,
  78
conference trade 8
crazy golf 21, 58
Cricketers, The 54
crime 90
Cultural Quarter 44
culture 12, 18
  around and north of
    Brighton Station 71–2
  city centre 48–9
  seafront 61–2
cycling 40

D

dental treatment 91
directory 90–93
disabilities, travellers with
  93
Divalls Café 74–5
driving 33, 40
drugs subculture 33, 91

Due South 65
Duke of York's Picturehouse
  67, 76

E

eating and drinking 16–17
  around and north of
    Brighton Station 74–6
  city centre 51–4
  east along the coast 88
  Lewes 83
  seafront 62–5
emergencies 91
entertainment 18–19
Exceat 87

F

Fair 73
fairground 59
Fatboy Slim 18, 56
Fillers 83
film locations 12
Fish Bowl, The 54
fish 'n' chips 16, 26
fishing 21
Fishing Museum and
  Gallery 61–2, 64
Fishing Quarter 27, 58
flea market 72
Font, The 55
Food for Friends 51
football 20–21
free attractions 30
Funky Buddha Lounge 65

G

gay community *see* LGBT
  community
George IV 11, 49
Glitterball 66
Gold Arts 50
Grand, The 24, 25, 58–9
Grapevine, The 23
Gulliver's 23
Guttersnipe Clothing 74
Guy Fawkes' Day 82

H

health emergencies 91
history 10–11
Honey Club 66
Horatio's 62
horse racing 21
hostels 22–3

Hotel du Vin 24–5
Hotel Seattle 24
hotels 23–5

I
itineraries 28–9

J
Jam Brighton 55
Jurys Inn 23

K
karaoke 66
Kemptown 22
Komedia 76, 78

L
Laine Deli 75
Lanes, The 14, 16, 26, 36, 46
Lewes 80–83
Lewes Castle 81–2
LGBT community 6, 9, 18
Lodestar Café 63
Long Man of Wilmington 87
Love Fit Café 52

M
Madeira Drive 22
maps 34–5, 43, 84
   symbols 4
medical treatment 91
Monk's House 87–8
Montezuma 50
Moo Moos 63
Moonrakers 88
Moshi Moshi 53
museums 12, 27, 48–9, 61–2, 71–2, 81

N
Naked Tea and Coffee Co 52
Nia 75
nightlife
   around and north of Brighton Station 76, 78
   city centre 54–5
   seafront 65–6
North Laine 14, 16, 27, 67–8, 72

O
Old Penny Arcade Museum 62
Old Steine 47
opening hours 92
orientation 36, 38

out of town
   east along the coast 85–8
   Lewes 80–83

P
Painting Pottery Café 75
Palm Court Restaurant 63–4
park and ride 33
Park View, The 78
parking 33
parks and gardens 47, 68
Paskins Town House 24
Pelham House 83
police 33
Preston Manor 68–9
Preston Park 68
public transport 38, 40
pubs 54, 62–3, 78, 88

R
reading, background 93
Regency Restaurant 65
Regency Square 22
restaurants 51–4, 63–5, 75–6, 83, 88
Revenge 55
reverse bungee 21, 58
Riddle & Finns Champagne & Oyster Bar 53–4
road, arriving by 33
rock 16
Rockery, The 68
Rodmell 87–8
Royal Pavilion 7, 11, 27, 46–7

S
safety and security 33, 90–91
St Bartholomew's Church 69–71
St Peter's Chapel 68
St Peter's Church 70
Sea Life Centre 60
seafront 56–66
seasons 8
Seven Dials 76
Seven Sisters 79, 86
Sheepcoat Valley Caravan Club Site 23
Sheridan Cooper's Wine Cellar 50

shopping 14–15, 49–50, 72–4, 92
skateboarding 58
slot machines 21
South Downs 27, 85–8
Southover Grange 82–3
spas 21
sport and relaxation 20–21
swimming 21, 58, 91
symbols 4

T
taxis 40
TFI Lunch 51, 76
Thatcher, Margaret 25
Theatre Royal 55
theatres 18, 48, 55
Three Jolly Butchers 78
Tictoc Café 52
Toast in Brighton 75
toilets 92
tombstoning 91
tourist information 93
trains 32–3, 90
travel
   to Brighton 32–3, 90
   within Brighton 38, 40

U
Umi 24

V
Victoria Fountain 47
Victoria's Bar 62–3
Volk's Bar & Club 66
Volk's Electric Railway 39, 61

W
watersports 21
Wax Factor, The 74
West Pier 61
wet weather attractions 31
White House Brighton, The 25
Woolf, Virginia 87–8
World Famous Pump Room 63

Z
Zafferelli 51

ACKNOWLEDGEMENTS

The photographs in this book were taken by Paul Cooper and Stuart Jackson for Thomas Cook Publishing, to whom the copyright belongs, except for the following:
Dreamstime page 9 (Paulpmp), page 20 (Gvision), page 29 (Adam Rauso), pages 44, 81 (Arun Bhargava), page 57 (Martinturzak);
Duke of York's Picturehouse page 77; iStockphoto page 29 (Tom Fewster), page 79 (Deborah Benbrook), page 86 (Geoff Blackmore)

Project editor: Thomas Willsher
Copy editor: Lucilla Watson
Proofreaders: Jan McCann & David Salkeld
Layout: Julie Crane
Indexer: Marie Lorimer

AUTHOR BIOGRAPHY

Debbie Stowe is a freelance journalist, travel writer and author. She has written over a dozen non-fiction and travel books, specialising in Indian Ocean and Eastern European destinations. Her writing also covers the natural world, film, human rights, and cultural and social issues. She lives in Bucharest.

Send your thoughts to
books@thomascook.com

- Found a great bar, club, shop or must-see sight that we don't feature?
- Like to tip us off about any information that needs a little updating?
- Want to tell us what you love about this handy little guidebook and more importantly how we can make it even handier?

Then here's your chance to tell all! Send us ideas, discoveries and recommendations today and then look out for your valuable input in the next edition of this title.

Email the above address (stating the title) or write to:
pocket guides Series Editor, Thomas Cook Publishing, PO Box 227, Coningsby Road, Peterborough PE3 8SB, UK.